£1·25

Staffordshire Portrait Figures

John Hall

Staffordshire Portrait Figures

Charles Letts and Company Limited

Published by
Charles Letts and Company Limited

Head Office:
Diary House, Borough Road, London, SE1

Publishing Consultant: Lionel Leventhal

Designed by: Kenneth Farnhill

Photographs: Michael Dyer Associates Limited

First Published 1972
Standard Book Number: 85097 050 4
Printed in Great Britain by William Clowes & Sons Limited.
London, Beccles and Colchester

Contents

Staffordshire Portrait Figures

INTRODUCTION

Ever since I decided to specialize in Staffordshire pottery figures I have always enjoyed, and learned more, from well illustrated books than from those devoted mainly to technical explanations about methods of manufacture and speculations involving the exact dating or the particular potter. When I was asked to contribute to this series I had already grown accustomed to giving information to those of my clients who were preparing books of their own. It was, therefore, only the knowledge that all the plates would be in colour that caused me to accept the invitation, because, next to being able to handle a particular piece, looking at a colour-plate of it is the best way to learn how to distinguish between the various semi-translucent glazes and opaque enamelled colours used by the potters in the period covered.

This book is offered, therefore, as a coloured pictorial companion to the many erudite tomes on the subject already available. It is a chronological presentation of the examples illustrated and, I hope, a text which will please veteran collectors and encourage tyros to be brave.

Lead Glazed Figures of the Eighteenth Century

It is strange to realize that a potter whose early works now command enormous prices should be known only by his surname and town. 'Astbury of Shelton' could refer to several men with this name who were working in Staffordshire from 1720 onwards, but it is possible that the most important of these was a John Astbury, who introduced the first lead-glazed red stoneware to England after allegedly learning the secrets of potting unglazed stoneware from two immigrant Dutch brothers, while pretending to be an idiot during the two years he worked for them.

It is thought that these brothers, John Philip and David Elers, came to England in 1688 with the court of William of Orange. Although their type of work pre-dates the illustrated content of this book it is interesting to note that it was their passion for secrecy, employing only dull-witted workmen, which paved the way to Astbury's eventual importance. One of his innovations, for example, was that in 1720 he added ground calcined flints to the lightest clay mixture then available and produced a white stoneware body that was hard, durable and easy to mould. Prior to this discovery most stone or earthenware bodies, then made from plastic clay and sand, had colours which ranged from light brown through red to black.

The early Astbury figures (known, to be absolutely correct, as salt-glazed stoneware) are mainly soldiers, mounted horsemen, musicians or groups of figures seated in a pew or on a high-backed bench. Primitive in appearance, these figures were produced from simple moulds finished with a great deal of hand modelling. They were made in coloured clays, sometimes decorated with browns, greens and greys under the final lead glaze. Whether they are the creations of John, or of his son Thomas Astbury, is still in doubt—but recently an Astbury pew-group in far-from-perfect condition has been priced at £10,000.

The next potter of note is Thomas Whieldon, who began his career sometime before 1740 as a manufacturer of tableware. Plates are typical examples of his work and the illustration on page 16 is included to show the extensive range of his palette. These coloured glazes, which could be fired at a very high temperature, were achieved by the use of metallic oxides. Yellow was obtained from ochre, brown and purple from manganese, blue and grey from cobalt, orange from iron and green from copper. The glazes blended together to give what is usually referred to as the appearance of tortoiseshell but, in my opinion, hand marbled-paper would provide a better and more realistic simile. The random application of colours ensures that every Whieldon plate and each piece of marbled-paper remains unique.

The Wood Family

Some of the most excellently modelled and delicately coloured English pottery figures were produced during the last half of the eighteenth century (1745–1795) by the Woods of Burslem. This famous father, brother and son partnership employed a similar, but more subtle, range of coloured glazes to those used by the Astbury-Whieldon group of potters. The elder Ralph Wood was apprenticed to John Astbury in 1730 and at the end of his training went to work for Thomas Whieldon, where he was able to experiment with the coloured glazes developed by his masters. His brother, Aaron, was apprenticed to Dr. Thomas Wedgwood and became the foremost modeller and blockmaker of his time.

The Wood glazes are semi-translucent—the result of diluting metallic oxides with the blueish-white glaze obtained from lead and, instead of the haphazard blending of the Astbury-Whieldon school, each colour was separately and carefully painted on by brush. Whilst all the figures produced by the Woods of Burslem are notable for the quality of modelling and the precision of their moulding not all of them are coloured. Many exist in white glost—a state, incidentally, which only serves to highlight their perfection.

The Woods were the first English potters to place signatures upon their works in the form of impressed capitals, R. WOOD for the father and Ra. WOOD BURSLEM for those items produced by his son. A rebus mark in the form of a group of three trees was occasionally used and some of the figures were impressed with mould numbers. Nevertheless marked specimens are very rare and I suspect that the examples which do occur were particularly signed in order to establish copyright in a large community where almost every other person was a potter. The output of many small manufacturers has been deprived of a place in the history

8

f ceramics because of this habit of 'borrowing' or copying from each other, which makes definite attribution of each piece produced at that time so difficult a task today.

Some examples of early Ralph Wood figures do appear with overglaze enamel decorations—a method of colouring figures which was developed towards the end of the eighteenth century. Most of these bear impressed numbers from known Ralph Wood moulds but the type of decoration reveals their later origin. Others, including busts of Handel, Milton and Sarah Siddons and figures of Chaucer, Newton and Shakespeare were later creations of Ralph Wood Junior and were issued only in the white glazed state or with overglaze enamel colours. All figures of this type which are decorated with a mixture of semi-translucent glazes and overglaze enamel colour—or with overglaze colours used discreetly (that is sparsely and with great effect which must be termed 'taste') should be attributed to Ra. WOOD BURSLEM and dated as products of the last three or four years before his early death, at the age of forty-eight, in 1795.

Were it not for the fact that underglaze coloured earthenware and figures come first in the hierarchy of potting it would be possible to continue the history of the Wood family here. But Enoch, son of Aaron, must await his proper place.

Pratt Ware

Pratt Ware (Plates 7, 8, 57 & 61) is a type of underglaze coloured earthenware, made in a great many places from Staffordshire to Sunderland between 1780 and 1830. The name is generic although originating from William Pratt and it ensures that dealers and clients the whole world over can discuss a 'Pratt' figure and know the term refers to a particular palette and a distinctive style of decoration.

All marked items are rare but the rarest mark on any of them is, strange to relate, that of William Pratt who was working in Fenton c. 1775–1810. These are by no means the best examples of this ware! Many other marks are recorded including those of Barker of Yorkshire, Emery of Mexborough, Dixon, Austin & Co. of Sunderland and Ferrybridge in Leeds.

The technical development to be noted here is that the colours were painted or sponged directly on to the earthenware body and fixed by firing before the piece received its final coating of white lead glaze and final firing.

The size of this book does not permit me to include more of the illustrations demanded by my enthusiasm for Pratt Ware. Another volume must be devoted to the many examples of animals, candlesticks, cornucopiae, dishes, figures, flasks, jugs, mugs, plaques (although I have shown a few of these in a later chapter), tea-caddies, teapots, vases and watchstands produced by the potters known as Pratt.

It must be noted that the younger Ralph Wood utilized this new method of decoration and that many of his figures, from moulds both old and new, were issued with typical Pratt colours. The plaque of Garrick (see Plate 60) is decorated in this style and may have been issued soon after his death in 1779.

Overglaze Enamelling

To continue the Wood Saga; a decade before the end of the eighteenth century
one of the talented (but unknown, therefore unsingable) potters realized that i
colours were applied after the piece had received its first white glazing the colour
range was greater and could be fired at a much lower temperature. It has been
suggested that this important advance in technique, known as Overglaze Enamel
ling, is also attributable to the young Ralph Wood. In my opinion, however, n
reasonable or conclusive evidence of a convincing nature has yet been submitted
The new process did, however, result in the separation of the men from the boys
Master potters employed it with discretion. Some, indeed, only used overglaze
colours if they could not obtain the same effects with coloured glazes or under
glaze colours. The others slapped it on like whores putting on make-up before a
rose-tinted mirror in a candle-lit room whilst preparing to take a walk in the sun
Prostitutes are often glorious and eternal but posterity properly ignores th
commonplace.

Two of the first potters to utilize the new technique of overglaze colouring wer
undoubtedly Enoch and his cousin, Ralph Wood the younger. Enoch, a yea
younger than Ralph, had begun modelling at the early age of eighteen. This is no
surprising when one remembers that his father, Aaron, was a master modeller and
must have given his son a wealth of technical know-how as well as providing hir
with a sterling example of ability.

It is my opinion, however, that Enoch Wood is more notable as a sculptor tha
as a potter. For this reason I have included nothing which can be positively attri
buted to him with the exception of his magnificently sculpted busts (Plate 56
Much of the other work blamed upon him falls into the prostituted or over-over
glazed enamel range I have already deplored. But, all in all, he was a remarkabl
man. He lived to be over eighty and fathered twelve children.

When Ralph's death brought their partnership to an end Enoch entered int
another with James Caldwell. They used the mark WOOD & CALDWELL bu
in 1819, he bought Caldwell out of the business and, as ENOCH WOOD & SONS
took some of his own progeny as partners.

Enoch Wood was also one of the first collectors of Staffordshire pottery. H
held a unique position in this field—being able to acquire rare examples not onl
from his father and uncle but also from his tutors and his rivals. On his death, i
1840, this collection was dispersed and no catalogue, alas, exists to delight and er
lighten the collector of today.

Other early enamel coloured figure makers include John Walton (Plates 1(
40 & 41) Obadiah Sherratt (Plates 11, 12, 13, 51 & 55) Lakin & Poole (Plate 14
John Cartledge, James Neale and Ralph Salt. Although no figure attributed t
Obadiah Sherratt has yet been found with a mark, all the other potters mentione
did occasionally sign their works. Walton and Salt used impressed or raise
capitals in a scroll applied to the back of the figure whilst Lakin & Poole and Neal
impressed various forms of their names beneath the figure's base. It is importar
to realize that even in this comparatively later period signed pieces were the e>

ception and never the rule. Many items can only be attributed to particular potters on stylistic grounds alone—unless one has marked and unmarked examples of the same figure to provide proof positive.

Charles Tittensor of Shelton was another early nineteenth century craftsman who sometimes signed his creations. Semi-translucent coloured glazes continued to dominate the decoration of his groups. A figure which is typical of his rare marked examples is shown on Plate 9.

Obadiah Sherratt

Obadiah Sherratt of Hot Lane, Sneyd Green, near Burslem, was born in 1775. It is said that he became a potter in 1810—although it seems unlikely that he would have waited until he was thirty-five before embarking upon a new career. He married Anne Davenport in 1797 and, at the time of her death in 1810, was listed as the owner of a potbank employing his wife and three children in the manufacture of earthenware toys. Both bride and groom, by the way, signed the register with a cross—an indication of illiteracy which perhaps accounts for some of his amusingly mis-spelt titles like 'Abram Stop' and 'Who Shall Ware The Breeches'.

Two months after Anne's death he married again, and Martha Austin became his second wife and workmate. This partnership flourished for the next thirty-six years and was notable for the many robustly modelled groups—more secular than sacred—which remain to remind us of English life during the Regency, the reign of William IV and the first decade of the Victorian era.

This escape from the mainly bucolic, mythological and religious output of his contemporaries paved the way for the equally spirited creations of the Victorian potters. Sherratt, in fact, was the modeller of the first truly Victorian figure, as, even before 1836, he had issued a figure, based upon an engraving in the *Dramatic Magazine*, of the beautiful and popular opera singer Maria Malibran. In September 1836, a few weeks after she fell from a horse, Malibran died, tragically, at the early age of twenty-eight. Opera lovers will appreciate the importance of this tragedy if they equate it with the loss of musical magic we should have suffered if Joan Sutherland had died in a car accident before February 17th, 1959, when she sang her first *Lucia di Lammermor* to one of the most overwhelming ovations ever offered by a grateful public.

In June 1837, Victoria came early and unexpectedly to the throne. Obadiah, probably prompted by Martha, took advantage of the superficial resemblance between Malibran and the young queen—mainly expressed in the hairstyle—to re-issue the figure with the addition of a pillar surmounted by a crown and the title HER MAJESTY QUEEN VICTORIA replacing the earlier one MALIBRAN. So far only one authenticated version of each figure has been recorded.

Victorian Staffordshire Figures

The figure of Isaac Van Amburgh (Plate 20) is the subject of special discussion in its caption. Whilst undoubtedly Victorian—because this Kentucky American made his English début at Astley's Amphitheatre in 1838—it defies provenance. If Sherratt had used gilt script and porcelaneous clay it could have been worthily ascribed to him. It remains, however, a magnificent enigma.

Thomas Balston wrote, about the earlier Victorian figures, 'for the sake of convenience, I propose to call them the 'Alpha' factory'. Despite all the research instigated by current experts no-one has succeeded in putting a name to the 'Alpha' potter, so I can only repeat what Balston wrote:

'At least twenty-three figures, all sitting or standing, can be readily recognized as products of the one [the "Alpha"] factory . . . All the contemporaries can be confidently dated from 1845 to 1851, and the historical figures are so similar in style that they are likely to be of the same period. All are modelled and painted in the round (there are no flat-backs among them), and are so complicated in design as to need at least three moulds. Captain Cook [Plate 23], the most complicated requiring eight.' He goes on to say that 'sixteen of the known figures are titled with indented capitals, with a gilt leaf or three strokes of gold paint at each end of the lettering; the others have a gilt line half way up across the front of the base and descending to the bottom of the base on each side. . . . All are so well modelled, moulded and painted that they are frequently offered for sale as Rockingham.'

Rockingham items, by the way, are usually marked, so beware of any unmarked Staffordshire porcelaneous figure offered for sale as Rockingham unless the person who is selling it is willing to provide an itemized account which includes circa dates and factory. There are a surprising number of people who refuse, or are unable, to authenticate the things they wish to sell.

Three of the most important dates in the annals of identification of Victorian portrait figures and their potters occurred in 1944, 1958 and 1963. In 1944 Raymond Mander and Joe Mitchenson, those indefatigable collectors and collators of theatre history, discovered that seven Shakespearian figures were based on engravings published in Tallis's *Shakespeare Gallery* (The London Printing and Publishing Co., 1852–1853). The prints proved that these figures were portraits of known actors and actresses and not imaginary representations of Shakespearian characters.

1958 saw the publication of the late Thomas Balston's *Staffordshire Portrait Figures of the Victorian Age* mentioned above. This important pioneer investigation into the processes of manufacture, designers, markets and prices was presaged by a beautifully illustrated article, 'Victorian Staffordshire Portraits', which he had written for *Country Life Annual* in 1951. The book, notable for its catalogue of portrait figures, will not only remain the classic example of original and enthusiastic research in this field, but has already provided other writers with an almost unchangeable formula for publications incorporating later discoveries. The importance of the 1963 date is connected with Balston's proposal of another name, 'Tallis', for those figures which matched in characteristics those already identified by Mander & Mitchenson. He noted, in his 1958 book: 'The moulds of very many 'Tallis' figures, not only portraits, are now in the possession of William Kent (Porcelains) Ltd., by whom many of them are still employed. This firm was not founded until 1878, and therefore cannot be the original makers of the portrait igures except Gordon, since the others all date from 1849–67.' This is followed by a footnote:

'William Kent Ltd. have kindly informed me that they do not know how they acquired the moulds. At some date they bought moulds from William Machin of Hanley, but he, according to Mr. Haggar, flourished from 1875 to 1899, too late to have originated them.' Significantly, although hitherto overlooked or ignored he footnote continues:

'Gaskell, Kent and Parr were the predecessors of William Kent Ltd. in the works in Aukland Street (late Wellington Street), Burslem, which they have occupied ever since their foundation in 1878. One John Parr, already a maker of 'toys' in 1860, had moved into these works in 1875, and is likely to be the Parr in this partnership. There had been Parr 'toy'-makers at Burslem, Richard (c. 1828), William (c. 1860) and Edward (c. 1860–4). It may have been through their connection with the Parrs that the Kents acquired the moulds.'

It was this connection which was important, and everything which pointed the way to the 1963 discovery was there in his book and unnoticed by me until December, 1967. At this time I was told that Tom Balston who had, alas, died in the October of that year, had bequeathed to me not only the copyrights to his books on Staffordshire figures but also his lifetime's notes and correspondence on the subject. Apart from his invaluable annotations, the letters alone were in hundreds from advanced collectors and specialist dealers, and not forgetting the owners of perhaps only one or two unique items.

But the Balston Archives were treasure indeed. One of the most important letters was from that erudite authority on British Ceramic Marks, Geoffrey Godden. It requests approval and permission to publish an article based upon Tom's book and his recent gift, to The National Trust, of nearly 450 Victorian Staffordshire portrait figures. These, by the way, are on loan to Lord Gretton, and housed at his country seat Stapleford Park, Melton Mowbray, Leicestershire, where they can be viewed.

The article, subsequently published in the *Pottery Gazette And Glass Trade Review* (May 1963), revealed, in Mr. Godden's usual informative and interesting prose, the following pedigree of Toy and Novelty Manufactures working in Burslem which he had discovered after reading Tom Balston's footnote:

> Richard Parr Junior (c. 1828–1835)
> Thomas Parr (working from 1852–1870)
> Kent & Parr (c. 1880–1894)
> William Kent (c. 1894–1944)
> William Kent (Porcelains) Ltd.
> (1944 . . . until they ended production in December 1962).

Since it is a well-known fact that the William Kent firms owned and used the original 'Tallis' moulds Mr. Godden submits—and I think he should have concluded—that Thomas Parr, a potter working at the time when the Mander & Mitchenson and Balston 'Tallis' items were issued, was the veritable creator of some of the finest mid-nineteenth-century figures ever created.

Such is the development of knowledge in any field—a pioneer's footnote becomes his posthumous chapter! How long will it be, however, before collectors and dealers stop thinking in terms of 'Tallis' for early and 'Kent' for later productions from the same moulds? Perhaps the traditional description, like the 'guinea' at Christies, will remain for ever.

Other types of figures illustrated are discussed in their captions or the adjoining text.

I am most grateful to those antique dealers and private collectors who have permitted examples in their stocks or collections to be photographed for inclusion in this book. I am particularly grateful, too, to those of our clients who brought items long distances, permitted us to delay delivery or purchased items after they had been photographed. I must add a special dedication to those who will eventually own the remaining items!

Valuable information culled from the published works or investigations of other authorities has been fully acknowledged in the text. I owe a special debt of gratitude to the late Thomas Balston, O.B.E., M.C., not only for favouring me with his friendship and patronage during the last decade of his long and productive life but also for his consideration in entrusting to me the archives relating to his treasured collection upon his death.

It would be an impertinence to commend the photographs when their excellence is so obvious. But I am grateful to those responsible for producing them who showed me how Staffordshire figures can be more magnificent in solitary splendour than even I, making my living from selling them, ever imagined.

Finally I must thank my partner, David MacWilliams, who not only told me that I must begin this book but provided me with enough tranquillity during business to enable me to finish it.

Plate 2 Astbury-Whieldon Man, possibly an actor. c. 1750. Height 8¾″

The suggestion that this figure represents an actor is based upon the fact that it greatly resembles, in style and colouring, a rare Astbury-Whieldon figure of Colley Cibber, actor and Poet Laureate (1671–1757), and, in form, a Bow figure of Henry Woodward (1714–1777) as the Fine Gentleman in Garrick's satire, *Lethe*. Although the play (Garrick's first) was produced at Drury Lane in 1740, this character was not introduced until the revised production of 1749. The Bow figure is based on a mezzotint by McArdle, published in 1750 after the painting by Francis Hayman, R.A.

Courtesy of Messrs. Jellinek & de Vermouthier

15

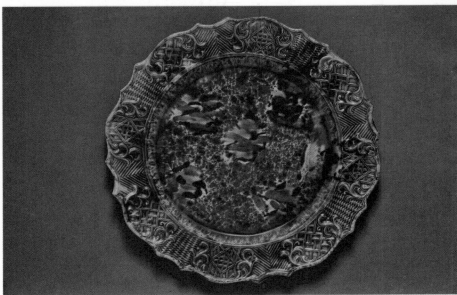

Plate 3 Whieldon Plates. c. 1750. Diameter 9″

16

Plate 4 Whieldon Performing Animals Group. c. 1760. Height $6\frac{1}{2}''$, Length $6\frac{3}{4}''$

Plate 5 Neptune. R. WOOD.
1750–1785. Height 8⅝″

A list of mould or subject numbers
known Ralph Wood productions
published in Frank Falkner's *The Woo
Family of Burslem*. Many of the
figures were issued with or without
pedestal on which the mould numb
was usually impressed. In this ca
mould number 22 is described
'Neptune on a Pedestal. 10¼‴'. The ear
number clearly indicates an origin
production of Ralph Wood Senior b
this item has been dated 1750–1785
cover the period when it would I
decorated in the semi-translucent glaz
illustrated here. Figures from the san
mould were produced later but the
were coloured with overglaze enamel

In the collection of Mr. Charles Smart

Plate 6 Toby Jug. Ra. WOOD BURSLEM (Impressed mould number 65). c. 1765–1795. Height $11\frac{1}{2}''$

These two examples of the works known to be by the Woods of Burslem —Neptune is from a mould numbered 22—have been chosen to show not only a range of their semi-translucent coloured glazes, but also to illustrate the difference between the careful application of their decoration and the haphazard blending typical of the Astbury-Whieldon School. (See Plates 2, 3 and 4.)

A type of stoneware beer-pot made in the first half of the seventeenth century, known as Bellarmine, is said to be the original of the Toby Jug. The neck of the pot, above a fat belly, is supposed to be a crude representation of Cardinal Roberto Bellarmino whose death, in 1621, delighted the Protestant potters of the Netherlands where he had instituted a campaign of religious persecution. This type of pot was current all over Europe. About the year 1765, however, some of England's leading potters produced a series of drinking vessels modelled as jolly (and usually seated) human beings. Aaron Wood is thought to be the inventor of the Toby Jug in this form and since some of the earlier jugs of this type are undoubtedly by the Woods of Burslem, for whom he was blockmaker, this is possible.

Many people think the Toby Jug was the drinking vessel. It was, in fact, only the container for the beverage. The detachable crown of the usually tricorne hat—as often missing from available examples as the pottery watches from the watchstands—was the actual cup. (See page 21.)

Plate 7 Sailor and Girl. Pratt Ware. c. 1805. Height 7″

The body glaze of 'Pratt Ware' is usually white, sometimes slightly tinged with blue depending upon its lead content. The palette is limited to oxide colours—browns, blues, greens, oranges, yellows and black—which would withstand the heat necessary to use the glaze. The Nelsonian sailor and his girl are two of the most completely decorated figures of this type I have seen and the brilliant yellow is at once the most beautiful and rare in the range.

The tufts of grass on the base (sometimes known as 'parsley') were produced by pressing clay through a fine sieve and applying small amounts of the resultant shreds to the figure with a knife. The same technique is used to provide the ermine edges of cloaks—such as that on the group of Eugenie and the Prince Imperial (Plate 28).

Courtesy of Messrs. Sampson & Seligman

Plate 8 Watchstand. Pratt Ware. Dixon, Austin & Co. c. 1827. Height 11″

Identical watchstands of this type are seldom seen, the assembly of supporters and applied decoration and the distribution of colour being so varied. The pottery watch, an important part of the original and which was sold with each of these items, is so often missing that examples are extremely rare. Presumably, when the watchstand was put into use and a real watch was inserted, the ceramic version was given to a child as a toy. This may account for a great deal of breakage and the resultant scarcity.

Plate 10 Crucifixion Group. Joh
Walton (impressed). c. 1818. Height 9

In the collection of Mrs. Thorneley Gibs

In the collection of Mr. Christopher Bibby

Plate 9 Town Crier. Charles Tittensor. c. 1815. Height 5½″

This figure is not only the earliest I have seen with this form of titling but it als
bears the longest (and most amusing) caption I have been able to record:

'LOST. On the first day of last term. Lawyer's consience!!
Whoever finds the same & brings it to the Crier, will receive the
handsome reward of six shillings and eight pence.'

Six shillings and eight pence, of course, has long been the supposed fee imposed b
every lawyer for each breath he draws on behalf of a client.

The semi-translucent coloured glazes are typical of the very rare specimer
marked 'Tittensor'.

Plate 11 'The Death of Munrow'. Obadiah Sherratt. c. 1810. Height $10\frac{1}{2}$",
Length $12\frac{1}{2}$"

The 'Munrow' preserved for posterity in this vigorous example of Sherratt's
invention was Lieutenant Hector Monroe, who met his feline fate near Calcutta
on December 2nd, 1792. The pedestal-type base is one immediately associated with
this potter's work, but the novelty of this piece is the black Bengal tiger which
replaces the yellow and black striped predator which usually dominates this group.

24

Plate 12 Bull Baiting Group. Obadiah Sherratt. c. 1830. Height 9″, Length 12½″

The bull baiting group is more often found on the pedestal-type base, when it is usually titled, 'BULL-BEATING. NOW CAPTAIN LAD', in two applied oval lozenges. Captain would be the dog who is being admonished to make greater efforts at beating or baiting the bull. It is possible to obtain versions of this group also on the pedestal base, which are about 8″ long and 6″ high, but most of these are too ill defined and badly decorated to be true Sherratt. It is possible that they were produced in the Kent & Parr or William Kent workshops.

Some researchers postulate that Sherratt's chimney ornaments were completely hand-modelled, the various units being shaped by rolling, cutting, pinching and, finally, tooling to accentuate the details. It is quite easy, however, to see the joint-line of a two-piece mould on the larger figures. Apart from this we have handled several broken examples where the evidence of fingerprints and slip-jointing inside the figures denotes definite hand-pressing from moulds.

Plate 13 'The New Marriage Act'. Obadiah Sherratt. Originally c. 1822. Heigh 6″, Length 6¼″

Another type of Sherratt base is illustrated above. A group which is thought to be of a fairly definite date, because of the event depicted, can sometimes provide a pitfall for the new, or unwary, collector. Although the group on the left of this picture is very colourful, the colours are so typical of the Kent & Parr (1880–1894 palette that it is undoubtedly one of their productions. It has less life, less attention to decoration and is slightly smaller than its blue and white counterpart. This indicates either poor copy modelling or the preparation of a new master-mould which always involves shrinkage, from an original by Sherratt.

The blue and white decoration on figures of this period is at once attractive and unusual. I have noted it on not more than seven other items.

Plate 14 Hygieia. Lakin & Poole (impressed mark). c. 1791–1795. Height 11″

This impressed mark was used only during the five years mentioned above. A much wider range of colours could be used by this method of overglaze enamel decoration. When the coloured enamels were painted over a first white glaze the second firing was at a temperature low enough to permit great detail and variation without the risk of the colours blending. Other notable items produced by this partnership include 'Cephalus & Procris', 'Rinaldo & Armida' and 'The Assassination of Marat'. It is possible that other items with the same delicately painted marbled bases emanate from this factory.

Courtesy of Messrs. Sampson & Seligman

27

Plate 15 Lucrezia. Wood & Caldwell. c. 1810. Height 5″, Length 9½″

This figure is ascribed to Wood & Caldwell on stylistic grounds since it resembles in both form and modelling a pair of Mark Antony and Cleopatra impressed 'WOOD & CALDWELL'.

The late Major Cyril Earle, in his book *The Earle Collection of Early Staffordshire Pottery* (see page 80), illustrated this figure as a product of Lakin & Poole, but he did not say it was a marked example. Since he also illustrated a Cleopatra as possibly by the same manufacturers I would suggest that he may have been misled by the flat bases of the figures he illustrated. These are typical of Lakin & Poole but the crudely painted marbling on them is not.

Plate 16 Two versions of The Lost Sheep. c. 1830. Heights $7\frac{3}{4}''-8\frac{1}{2}''$

These figures derive from an original by Ralph Wood c. 1770. Examples of the type illustrated above are usually ascribed to Enoch Wood or James Neale but I have deliberately offered no attribution because they fall into the over-over-enamelled group described on page 10. The enormous amount of copying of ideas or actual models which took place has already been mentioned. Griselda Lewis states: 'Potters were always going out of business and sales of potteries were frequently advertised ... showing the whole stock-in-trade of a factory including moulds.'

Ignoring the square base, which adds the extra $\frac{3}{4}''$ height to one, careful comparison of the figures shows that two of the many different potters engaged in the manufacture of these items have made their own moulds of the sheep and the shepherd from an earlier Wood model. Only one of them has displayed any sign of originality by adding the dog and altering the shape of the base.

Plate 17 Toby Jug. John Liston as Paul Pry. Unknown potter. c. 1829. Height 5"
John Liston as Sam Swipes. Unknown potter. c. 1825. Height 6".

John Liston (1776–1846) was the most famous comedian of his day and from
about 1825 until he retired in 1837 numerous figures depicting him in many rôles
were issued by various potters. It is interesting to note that Garrick, an actor more
illustrious than Liston, was less often celebrated ceramically.

Although the figures were issued when Liston created the roles, his popularity
ensured that they were current throughout his career. The first night of John
Poole's play *Paul Pry* was September 13th, 1825, but the toby jug of Liston as
Paul Pry was more probably made for his appearance in the 1829 revival.

Another of his popular characters was Sam Swipes in Theodore Hook's *Exchange
No Robbery*. Whilst there are many figures of him in this character this example is
one of only two I have ever seen with such brilliant overglaze decoration.

Plate 18 Bear Baiting Jug. Morris, Stoke (impressed). Height 12½″

This cruel but imposing creation, typical of British sporting taste even in the early nineteenth century, is practical as well as decorative. The head of the bear is removable and forms a cup which can be filled, by the alcoholic beverage presumably contained in its body, through the mouth of the dog which forms the spout of the jug.

There seems to be no record of any potter named Morris working around 1800 to 1820 when I believe, from the subject and style of decoration, this piece was made.

Plate 19 'George & Dragon'. ?Wood & Caldwell. 1795. Height $14\frac{1}{2}''$
'St. George'. Unknown Potter. c. 1862. Height $11''$

There are at least seventeen different Staffordshire versions of our patron saint—
the most beautiful being a model which is sometimes impressed 'Ra. WOOD.
BURSLEM'. Shown here is a later version from the same mould, which not only
has a rare and interesting plinth-type base but is the only titled one I have recorded
earlier than Obadiah Sherratt.

The Illustrated London News for March 15th, 1862, provides the source of the
Victorian 'St. George'. The engraving depicts the central sculpture of the South
Fountain at Witley Court, Worcestershire. The subject of this group is Perseus, on
Pegasus, rescuing Andromeda from a sea monster. The monster could easily pass
for a dragon so the potter had only to ignore Andromeda and clip the wings of
Pegasus to provide yet another St. George to tempt the pockets of a patriotic public.

32

Plate 20 'Mr. Van Amburgh' (gilt script). Unknown potter. c. 1838. Height 6¾"

Just at the beginning of the Victorian age this superb confection was created by an unfortunately unknown genius who loved either Mr. Van Amburgh or the potter's art—most probably both. It has transcended the elaboration of the previous decade: it has no superfluous arabesques or bocage. Its very simplicity is so deceptive that more than one eminent documentor of Victorian Staffordshire portrait figures insists that it must have a great deal of modelling by hand. It has, indeed, a great amount of hand work . . . but only that provided by the Repairer. This was the name given to the workman who assembled the nineteen or twenty separate moulds prepared by this most prodigal potter for what must have been his *ièce de résistance*. Having had the opportunity to compare seven of these magnificent groups at the same time, and to inspect them thoroughly, it seems obvious to me that whilst each separate part is an exact replica of any other part from the same mould, the Repairer's assembly of the parts—involving slight changes of position here and there—can create a misleading impression of the unique.

In the collection of Miss Jean Anderson

33

Plate 21 (*left to right*) 'Douglas' (inscribed), c. 1821, height 7″; A wounded sergeant of the Staffordshire Regiment, c. 1820, height 6″; An officer of the 80th Staffordshire Volunteers, c. 1828, height 8″; A barber, c. 1820, height 6¼″; Billy Waters, c. 1821, height 7¼″

No definite attributions are offered as to the potters responsible for these superb small Staffordshire figures. All of them are decorated in overglaze enamel colours but whilst 'Douglas' and Billy Waters are typical of Obadiah Sherratt, the wounded sergeant and the barber both have bases which are known on pieces marked with the cartouches used by John Walton and Ralph Salt. The officer of the 80th Staffordshire Volunteers has a base which is common to so many manufacturers of the period that one would hesitate, in retrospect, to offend any of them by proposing one in particular as the possible creator.

Billy Waters was a beggar and itinerant musician who existed by playing his fiddle, like the busker of today, mainly in London's West End. He had a peg-leg and a companion known as African (or Black) Sall. She, I presume, collected money for him from good-natured passers-by, her only other recorded talent being euphemistically termed 'Good-Time Girl'.

The figure of Billy Waters is dated c. 1821 because it was during this year that Pierce Egan's book, *Tom & Jerry: Life in London* was adapted as an operatic extravaganza by W. T. Montcrieff, and produced at the Adelphi Theatre. Billy was engaged to appear in some of the crowd scenes, including one in a tavern and another at Hyde Park Corner. The production ran for almost 300 nights—a record long run which ended only because the principal actors were tired of it. The end of the run provided them with a well earned rest, but the loss of regular employment meant only poverty and a pauper's grave for Billy Waters. His birth is unrecorded and his death, in March 1823, might also have passed unnoticed had it not occurred so soon after the final curtain of this Adelphi extravaganza.

One feature of the figure chosen for this illustration is that he is shown with a white face. Billy Waters was a Negro and all other recorded examples exhibit his natural black complexion. Since racial prejudice was unimportant at the time the only possible explanation for the anomaly is that the decorator had used up his day's supply of overglaze black before consigning this particular image to the kiln.

The white example in the collection of Mr. Arthur Thornton

Plate 22 John Philip Kemble as Hamlet. Thomas Parr ('Tallis'). c. 1852. Height 11″

The uncoloured Hamlet has passed through the clay (before firing) and biscuit (first firing) states and is at the glazed, or glost state. This means it has been dipped in the glaze-vat and re-fired in the glost oven. It is interesting to note that the feather on his hat is missing. This was obviously overlooked during all three processes because the joining points are also covered with glaze.

Imperfect pieces, known as 'wasters' were usually broken and thrown on to the factory rubbish-dump but a figure with such slight damage might be sold cheaply. A William Kent price-list c. 1901 reveals the wholesale price of this Hamlet to be ten shillings the dozen—so a waster would have been very inexpensive! It is most fortunate that this particular figure was not thrown away because it illustrates an important characteristic of 'Tallis' figures—that they never have colours under the glaze.

John Philip Kemble (1757–1823) made his first great success as Hamlet in Dublin in 1781 and chose the same rôle for his London début, at Drury Lane Theatre, in 1783. The fact that his image appears at all in this series of 'Tallis' Shakespearian characters is entirely due to the fact that one of the engravings in the *Shakespeare Gallery* was based upon Sir Thomas Lawrence's painting of Kemble as Hamlet which is now in the National Portrait Gallery, London.

Plate 23 Captain James Cook. 'Alpha' Factory. ?c. 1851. Height 7"

Most Victorian Staffordshire portrait figures can be confidently dated because of an event; a contemporary happening, a fiftieth, hundredth, one hundred-and-fiftieth or two hundredth anniversary of the subject's birth, death or principal achievement was often celebrated in pottery. The reason for the production of Captain Cook, however, remains obscure. Born in 1728, he became an able seaman in 1755, master seaman in 1759, captain in 1775 and he died in 1779. Nathaniel Dance painted the portrait from which this figure derives in 1776. None of these dates would, however, provide a major anniversary compatible with the period 1845–1851, which Thomas Balston has circumscribed for 'Alpha' figures. The only possible solution seems to be that it was specially created for the Great Exhibition of 1851, perhaps as a patriotic symbol of an expanding empire. In any case Captain Cook's image required at least eight moulds instead of the minimum three required by most 'Alpha' figures, so the occasion which demanded it was obviously very special.

In the collection of Miss Elizabeth Johnson

Plate 24 William Charles Macready as Macbeth. Thomas Parr ('Tallis'). c. 1852. The coloured version ?William Kent. ?c. 1900. Height 8¼″

In the collection of Mr. James Bree

The coloured Macbeth is not the worst example of a Kent reproduction I have seen and I do not believe it is one issued by William Kent (Porcelains) Ltd. during the period between the end of the Second World War, when they recommenced production of these figures, and 1962, when they ceased using the moulds. It is more likely to have been made c. 1900.

It is always wise, however, to insist on being given an invoice which incorporates circa dates and a full guarantee of authenticity. The tyro collector can be saved both money and misery by observing this rule to the letter as any reputable dealer is concerned with his good name and will never refuse to supply a detailed receipt.

A comparison of the 'Kent' and 'Tallis' specimens illustrates several points by which one can determine the correct date of issue. Some of the characteristics of Thomas Parr 'Tallis' figures, first proposed by Thomas Balston, but listed in my order of importance are as follows:

    (a) they are usually modelled and painted in the round,
    (b) they have no underglaze colouring,
    (c) their bases are coloured with 'combed' strokes of pale green, brown, yellow and orange,
    (d) all titles are in indented capitals or transfer-printed (in gold),
    (e) they are exceptionally heavy.

I would add:

    (f) all colours, including black, are delicately and economically applied.

The reproductions can be recognized by these additional observations:

    (g) the bases are coloured with blurred splotches of dark green and brown,
    (h) the indented capitals are faint and crudely filled in with black,
    (i) all colours are thickly, inefficiently and inartistically applied—iron red, the hallmark of reproduction, being predominant.

In short, the original decorators, economical in the application of colours, were working to live and reproducers were being subsidized to perpetuate a tradition.

Despite all the faults chronicled by today's experts, the final year's output of William Kent (Porcelains) Ltd. will still be antiques (in the legal sense) to the collector of 2062.

The coloured version in the collection of Mrs. Richard Cashmore

Plate 25 Charlotte & Susan Cushman as Romeo & Juliet. Thomas Parr ('Tallis') c. 1852.

Charlotte Cushman (1816–76) and her sister, Susan (1822–59) were American actresses born in Boston. They came to London in 1845 when they were wildly acclaimed for their performances as Romeo and Juliet. They remained in England appearing at many theatres in London and throughout the country, until 1849. They returned to delight English audiences again from 1852 until 1857.

This illustration shows the two types of decoration favoured by the 'Tallis' potter. Some collectors prefer the fully coloured examples whilst others take delight in the mainly white and gold versions. Both are equally desirable.

The title, in upper and lower case type, is:

> *Jul.*   O think'st thou we shall ever meet again?
> *Rom.*   I doubt it not; and all these woes shall serve
>   For sweet discourse in our time to come.

Later reproductions are crudely and thickly coloured and titled 'Romeo & Juliet' in clumsy gilt script.

Both in the collection of Mr. Harry Ryans

Plate 26 'J. J. Gurney' (gilt script). Unknown potter. c. 1847. Height 11¼″

The figure of Joseph John Gurney (1788–1847), banker, Quaker minister and philanthropist, has been chosen to illustrate the fine results obtained by the use of both underglaze and overglaze passages.

The blue is cobalt oxide applied beneath the glaze and the black is a compound of manganese, iron and cobalt mixed with vitreous flux and painted over the glaze before the final firing. It presents the matt appearance of cloth.

'Rev. Christmas Evans' (raised capitals). Unknown potter. Height 13½″

The brilliance of underglaze black is used to great advantage on this representation of the Rev. Christmas Evans (1766–1838), a Welsh farm-servant who became the chief minister of all the Baptist churches in Anglesey. His right eye was injured during a religious brawl in 1788. The only date I can suggest for manufacture is 1866, the centenary of his birth.

In the collection of Mrs. Thorneley Gibson

Plate 27 'Henry V Trying On The Crown' (raised capitals). Unknown potter. c. 1847. Height 13¾"

This magnificent figure is based on an engraving after a painting by John Calcott Horsley, in *The Illustrated London News* of September 25th, 1847. The title of the picture is: 'Henry V when Prince of Wales, when believing the King to be Dead, Takes the Crown from the Cushion'. It illustrates a point in the section on identification that the potter's source was usually an engraving rather than the original painting.

The Illustrated London News is a veritable well of source-material and among the many figures potted from its multitudinous wood-engravings— apart from those already mentioned— are Daniel O'Connell and Sir Robert Peel; Kossuth, the Hungarian Patriot; The Sultan of Turkey, Victor Emmanuel II and Garibaldi; Macready, as James V of Scotland in *The King of the Commons* and Ellen Bright, the young Lion Queen who was mauled to death during a performance of her act at Chatham.

Penny Plains and Twopence Coloured prints, those attractively stylized representations of actors and actresses in their favourite rôles also known as Toy Theatre prints, have inspired many models including Edmund Kean as Richard III, his son, Charles as Rolla in *Pizarro*, Macready as Rob Roy and Sarah Egerton as his Helen MacGregor.

Plate 28 'Empress of France' (raised capitals). Unknown potter. c. 1856. Height 12¾"

This is the tallest and most beautifully coloured example of this group I have ever seen. It represents Empress Eugenie (1826–1920), wife of Napoleon III of France, with their son, the Prince Imperial. Born in 1856, he was killed whilst fighting for England in the Zulu campaign of 1879.

In the collection of Mr. Harry Ryans

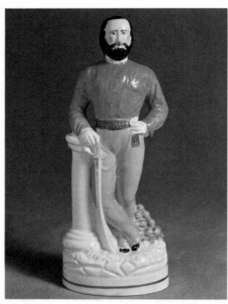

Plate 29 Giuseppe Garibaldi. Thomas Parr ('Tallis'). c. 1864. Height 8½″

Garibaldi (1807–1822), Italian soldier and patriot, visited England in 1864. He was welcomed with great enthusiasm and at least sixteen different figures of him are known to have been issued during that year.

In the collection of Mr. Adrian Wield

Plate 30 Generals French and Buller. Sampson Smith. c. 1899. Heights 12″

Most Staffordshire figures of this period were sparsely coloured but it is possible to discover such well-decorated and crisply-moulded items as the two illustrated here.

In the collection of Mr. Ronald Shockledge

The smaller figure in the collection of Mr. & Mrs. Duncan FitzWilliam

late 31 The Duke of Wellington. Unknown potters. *Left* c. 1852. Height 12″.
ight c. 1840. Height 6½″

Arthur Wellesley, First Duke of Wellington (1769–1852) was not only the most
mous British general of the nineteenth century but an eminent politician as well.
ɔ it is not surprising that he was so often celebrated in pottery.

The two items here show how proportion plays a great part in the formation of a
ɔllection. The same subject can be found in a variety of sizes, and if only one
xample of each person is required for your collection, Wellington is available
ɔm 3″ up to 18½″.

45

Identification

Apart from the figures identified by engravings already mentioned, building statues, paintings, photographs, postcards and, above all, music-fronts, have a provided positive identification of untitled portrait figures or proved to be th proper source of titled ones. Buildings and statues have led to the source or titli of such figures as Benjamin Franklin, John Wesley, Mozart and Robert Burns.

Paintings and photographs, again, usually after they have been engraved, a the source of many figures. Several of the 'Tallis' engravings were after Dague rotypes by Paine of Islington. Figures of Cook, Othello & Iago, 'Henry V Tryir On The Crown' and Kemble as Hamlet originate from prints after paintings. B postcards first revealed the origins of figures made after Sir Thomas Lawrence Master Lambton (The Red Boy) and Onslow Ford's statue of General Gordo

Other types of lithographs and engravings have provided source material fo figures of William IV, his consort Adelaide, and the Prince of Wales (later Edwa VII) on a Shetland pony; Maria Malibran and Madame Vestris, who was a notab actress and the first woman theatre manager and the Revd. Charles Spurgeo for whom the Metropolitan Tabernacle was erected and the Revd. John Fletche previously thought to be a figure of John Wesley holding a skull instead of th usual bible in his hand.

One tends to forget that before the advent of the radio, gramophone, motio picture or television, leisure time was filled with self, or home entertainment ar all members of an educated family were expected to be able to sing or to play son instrument well enough to entertain each other and their friends. This created great demand for sheet music: and publishers, from about 1800 to the end of th nineteenth century, soon discovered that a well-illustrated cover would sell even trite piece of music! They have thus provided us, by their enormous output engraved and lithographed music-fronts, with a fantastic record of world histor Every event, however absurd, comic, serious or tragic seems to have been cel brated in song or some instrumental arrangement.

On the first night of a new opera, for example, the publisher would secure sea for one of his artists and composers. The artist would sketch details of costum scenery and highlights of the performance whilst the composer (usually a hac musician) would note the melodic lines of the principal arias. Within a few days taking *La Traviata* as the particular first performance—the music shops would t filled with new publications, each with a beautiful portrait of a principal perform or illustrating some dramatic moment, variously titled 'The Traviata Valse'- quadrilles, polka or galop.

But everything was commemorated: royal accessions, weddings, births ar deaths; alliances and wars; politics, religion, sport and events of every nature. is for this reason that some of the most important, interesting and excellent drawn lithographs of the Victorian age still exist today. Like Staffordshire figure which are uniquely British, they provide a panorama of nineteenth-centu society unparalleled anywhere in the world. During the last ten years we ha identified twice as many figures from these as from all other sources combined.

Plate 32 Rebecca Isaacs. Thomas Parr ('Tallis'). c. 1851. Height 8½″
Music-front lithographed by Thomas Coventry.

Rebecca Isaacs (1829–1877) was a successful actress and vocalist. The song,
'I want to be a Bloomer' was introduced in *Follies of the Day* at the Adelphi
Theatre during the year of The Great Exhibition.

47

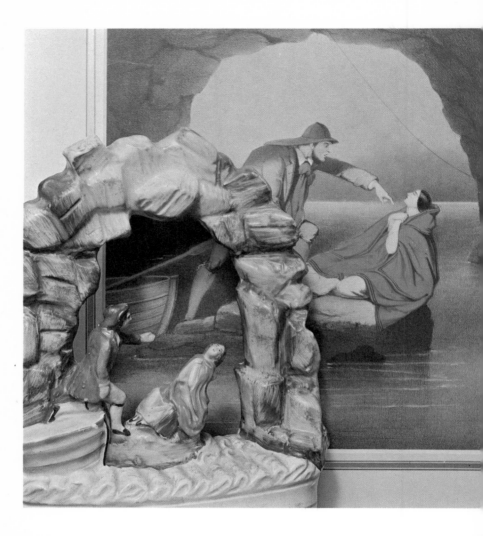

Plate 33 Edmund Falconer as Danny Man and Agnes Robertson as Eily O'Conner in *The Colleen Bawn*. Unknown potter. c. 1860. Height 9″
Music-front lithographed by John Brandard.

Agnes Robertson was the wife of the author of this play, Dion Boucicault, which was first produced in England at the Adelphi Theatre on September 10th, 1860.

Plate 34 Adelaide Kemble and Mrs. Alfred Shaw as Semiramide and Arsaces in Rossini's opera, *Semiramide*. Unknown potter. c. 1842. Height 6″
Music-front lithographed by John Brandard.

It will be noted that the figure is a mirror-image of the group depicted on the music-front. This may indicate that its real source is a pirated edition of Brandard's drawing since most of these are drawn on to the stone from an original edition so subsequent pulls are printed in reverse.

49

In the collection of Mrs.

Plate 35 ?Frederic Maccabe. Unknown potter. c. 1850. Height 8¼″
Music-front lithographed by M. & N. Hanhart.

These items have been selected to show the possibility that the figure r
Frederic Maccabe as 'The Troubador Of The Past' but they are not c
proof positive. There are, however, so many points of similarity bet
figure and the music-front that a line of further research is opened up. '
grapher may have exaggerated Maccabe's actual costume or, and thi:
likely, the potter has simplified it. Then again, an exact print may be d
which will finally determine the truth.

The watchstand in the collection of Mr. Anthony Vandervell

Plate 36 *Left to right:* Scotsman & Girl, possibly theatrical, ?c. 1855, height 8½″; Watchstand surmounted by an equestrian figure of an officer, a saint or a circus performer, ?c. 1850, height 10¼″; Two lovers, possibly theatrical, ?c. 1845, height 8″. Unknown potters.

After seeing thousands of Staffordshire figures over a number of years certain untitled items almost beg to be recognized before being sold! It could be the style of modelling, the type of base or decoration—or even the conviction that somewhere, sometime, one has seen a print which will provide the piece with a name and its right to an entry in a catalogue. The purely decorative Victorian Staffordshire figure is still considered a bastard by many collectors. Although such a piece may seem overpriced the wise collector will buy it, suspecting its changeling status, before the dealer is able to produce the proof of identity which will give him the right to raise the price again!

Plate 37 Two versions of an unidentified equestrienne, possibly theatrical. Unknown potter. ?c. 1847. Heights 12″ & 12½″

There is a third version of this figure, less elaborately modelled and only $10\frac{3}{4}$″ tall. All three are decorated in the same style and palette as a figure of Eliza Cook which is definitely a product of the 'Alpha' factory.

The reason for including this illustration is to draw attention to the marked differences between two items which, on cursory examination, might appear identical to the untrained eye. Colouring and slight variations in height may always be ignored (except when dealing with reproductions!) but, even though the faces are obviously the same, the open-necked blouse and loosely tied scarf on one is modelled as a high cravat on the other. The figure's identity has puzzled collectors for many years and she has been tentatively titled Dorothy Vernon, 'La Zingara', a circus equestrienne and Louisa Nisbett as Constance in *The Love Chase*.

The recent happy discovery of a figure which I have positively identified as Mrs. Nisbett as Constance (see Plate 38) might seem to narrow the choice of a name for these other items. But there is a painting, by James Godsell Middleton, of Mrs. Nisbett appearing in the same rôle at the Worthing Theatre Royal in 1838, and whilst she is depicted in a different costume, her face and hairstyle are so similar to the figures in riding habit that, unless another identification is made, one must continue to search for a print in which she wears her hair down in this scene.

Plate 38 Louisa Cranstoun Nisbett as Constance in *The Love Chase* (by James Sheridan Knowles). 'Alpha' factory. c. 1847. Height $7\frac{3}{4}''$
Page 256 of *The Illustrated London News* dated April 17th, 1847.

Louisa Nisbett (1812–1858), formerly Miss Mordaunt, began her stage career at Greenwich in 1828. Her great beauty, vivacity and acting abilities gained her considerable success in the provinces and London. In 1831 she temporarily retired from the stage on marrying Captain Nisbett who died only seven months later. In 1839 she married Sir William Boothby and upon his death, in 1846, again returned to the stage.

The illustration, which is the source of the figure, is from a report of her first reappearance on the stage of the Haymarket Theatre.

Quality, Condition and Rarity

Presumed rarity should never blind a collector to the quality and condition of a item he proposes to add to his collection. Quality, the cardinal virtue, followed b condition and then rarity are the prime factors which determine high prices. It more sensible to buy a superior item each month than to acquire an inferior on every week.

Apart from being representative of a particular period or potter all the figures i this book were selected for their quality. Comparison is simple when one object good and the other one awful (see Plate 42), but the two versions of The Cobble illustrated opposite, show how important it is to be able to recognize degrees excellence.

When the figure on the marbled base was first sold to Vern Miller, whose ex tensive collection is noted for superb quality and condition it was considered to b a fine enough piece. (There were many c. 1900 reproductions available at the tim —even at Antiques Fairs!) When, however, it was returned to us for repai having been broken during a struggle with a burglar, the sad conclusion wa reached that, by comparison with the figure on the black base, the Miller cobble is only fine whilst the other is superb.

Condition is the next point of importance and here we are mainly concerne with repairs and restorations. A repaired figure is one which has been broken an has had the original part put back. If it has been a simple break—such as a hea or a hand—the value is not much affected. A restored figure is one which has ha a missing part, or parts, remodelled and replaced and its value depends upon th extent and excellence of the restoration.

Some people refuse to collect damaged figures, especially those of the nineteent century, no matter how well they have been repaired or restored; but reasone consideration has convinced many others that certain figures are so rare that the proffered damaged example is basically fine it can but grace their collectio until or *if* a perfect one becomes available. Several of the most attractive an desirable figures recorded are, of course, either unique or known to exist in onl three or four collections.

A particular example is the 12″ figure of Sir Colin Campbell (No. 62f in Th Balston Collection at Stapleford Park) which was rescued from the dustbin of shop near Burnley. Some dealers reserve recent acquisitions for inspection b regular clients, so it is always worth enquiring whether there is anything of intere not on display. On this occasion the answer was 'I had a Colin Campbell thi morning but the bottom dropped out of my carrier-bag when I came into the shop

Further enquiry elicited the fact that Sir Colin had been consigned to the dust bin—as a 'cracked pot', a complete loss and entirely worthless. When the deale finally produced the disaster, the head of the figure clearly showed that it belonge to a figure which was previously unrecorded. The repairs were relatively costl but to this day, over ten years later, it remains the only known example of th figure.

Plate 39 Two examples of The Cobbler. Unknown potter. c. 1820. Heights 7″

The close-up highlights some of the detail. Note, for example, the folds of the shirtsleeve, the eyebrows, facial expression and the hair showing through the torn hat which, on the other version, appears untorn.

Version on marbled base in the collection of Mr. Vern K. Miller

Plate 40 Two examples of Moses. John Walton. c. 1820. Heights 11″

The main point illustrated here is that both figures are exactly as issued. They have no repairs or restorations. The Restorer (a term which originally designated the workman responsible for assembling the separately moulded parts) has so positioned the hands on the upraised arms that the owner of one might reasonably suspect the other to be false.

I would have written that both were perfect instead of 'as issued': but the secondary point, decoration, provides the reason why one has been delicately enamelled with great attention paid to detail and the other, in the red gown, has been heavily painted. This figure has been damaged during the preliminary stages of its manufacture—probably by being pushed against another object during the first firing. In consequence an area of about one inch square, commencing at the lowest frontal point of the blue and yellow cloak, and another, half an inch wide and two inches long, from the top of the left knee to the foot, have been depressed. These malformations, skilfully disguised by a clever decorator, could easily pass unnoticed.

Plate 41 'St. Peter' and 'St. Paul'. John Walton. c. 1825. Heights 9¾", 8"

Whilst these items demonstrate further points relating to quality and condition they belong equally to the following section about prices.

St. Peter is more than double the price of St. Paul. Granted they were originally issued as a pair it is immediately obvious that one row of bocage is missing from the figure of St. Paul. Since it is less expensive for the owner, and easier for the present-day restorer, such points of breakage are usually rounded-off and painted over. Inexperienced collectors might examine the head, hands and sword of this figure for signs of repair or restoration and, not knowing that it should have two rows of bocage, overlook the defect which would be apparent to the expert.

Bocage is often completely missing from figures and groups of this period. Some, indeed, have been endowed with layers of false leaves in an attempt to deceive: but incompetent restorers, like the manufacturers of reproductions, failed to notice that each leaf of genuine bocage is composed of two separate pieces, a front and a back, or, if they had noticed, were not prepared to spend time on the tedious process of stamping each leaf out of a flat bat of clay and the further time required for the delicate task of assembling them correctly.

It is wise to view with suspicion any bocage which is made in one large piece and even that with separate leaves which does not consist of two pieces noticeably laid back to back.

Plate 42 Two versions of a sailor. Unknown potters. c. 1900 & 1870. Heights
13″, 11½″

Despite the enormous amount of inferior Staffordshire figures available in shops
and auction rooms throughout the country I experienced great difficulty in ob-
taining the right items to illustrate this point. I was obliged, therefore, to abandon
exactitude and make do with figures of different sizes.

It is always advisable to reject any figure of bad quality—even though it is a
rarity at what seems to be a bargain price—because nothing of bad quality can
be a bargain. It is preferable to see a damaged, repaired or restored figure of fine
quality displayed, than a 'bargain' such as the sailor on the left.

*I have promised the obliging friend who lent me the monster that he shall remain anonymous, but I do acknowledge, with
gratitude, his courtesy in permitting me to photograph this ugly object.*

58

Plate 43 'Jenny Lind' (impressed capitals). 'Alpha' Factory. c. 1847. Height $7\frac{3}{4}''$

'M. Lind' (impressed capitals). 'Alpha' Factory. c. 1847. Height $8''$

Some Reasons For High Prices

Anybody who frequents auction rooms should have noticed that the proportion of sales announced for English Pottery and those devoted to English and Continental Porcelain are in the ratio of 1 : 7; and an inspection of almost any antique-district in the world will confirm the fact that fine pottery is much rarer than fine porcelain. With the exception of two plates, included to show the Whieldon colour-range (see Plate 3), table or other domestic wares are not included here, but fine examples of these are just as rare and desirable as figures of the same period.

Whilst there is a fantastic difference in the prices paid today for paintings of certain artists who were innovators—often despised during their lifetimes—and the products of master-potters of the eighteenth and nineteenth centuries, the relatively high prices now obtained for pottery are being given for exactly the same reasons; rarity and availability.

There are many gaps yet to be filled in museum collections but several desirable items, which have previously passed from private collection to private collection, have been irrevocably removed from the open market and incorporated into museum displays. Victorian Staffordshire is more often acquired by American museums than by those in England but certain provincial museum committees, including those of Bradford and York, are to be congratulated upon their foresight.

Christie's was the first saleroom to produce a catalogue devoted to Victorian Staffordshire figures in October 1963. They followed this by auctioning the first part of a further collection in October 1964. Four parts of this enormous accumulation have now passed through the same rooms. Since that time, whilst mediocrity has not been encouraged by the public, really good figures have increased in value from year to year.

Some figures which are by no means rare have always commanded higher prices than others equally fine and sometimes scarcer. The reason for this lies in the number of collecting categories into which the figure can be integrated. This can best be explained by listing those categories applicable to William Smith O'Brien (see Plate 46).

O'Brien was a Member of Parliament for County Limerick who, in 1848, started a revolution in the rural districts of Ireland and was convicted of high treason. Although he was sentenced to be hanged, drawn and quartered, his sentence was commuted and he was transported to Tasmania. It is an 'Alpha' figure and some people confine their collections to examples from this factory. He was also a politician, an Irishman, a criminal and had enforced connections with Australia— four other categories which are separately collected. Last, but not least, it is a fine figure sought after by all collectors of Staffordshire portraits. So there is one general and five specific types of collector who will bid against each other for possession of this item.

ate 44 'Miss F. Nightingale' (raised
pitals). Unknown potter. c. 1855.
eight 10½"

Florence Nightingale (1820–1910)
ell known as 'The Lady with the
amp' (although no Staffordshire figure
as been discovered showing her hold-
g one!) reached Scutari, in the Crimea,
th her nurses in 1854. Another figure
ows her attending a wounded officer
ut since her efforts were devoted en-
rely to improving the medical treat-
ent of other ranks this must be a fig-
ent of imagination on the part of the
otter. Three other different models, as
ell as a bust of her, are recorded, but
llectors must be warned that the
nallest, 5¼" figures standing with the
ft hand on a pedestal, are usually late
roductions of Kent & Parr or William
ent (Porcelains) Ltd.
Another representation of her,
therto overlooked, exists in a group
led 'The Soldier's Farewell'. This
picts a kilted Highland soldier in a
usby, supporting a sorrowful maiden
hose head droops on to his right
oulder. The maiden is, in fact,
lapted from the figure illustrated here.
I have seldom met a nurse or doctor
ho has not expressed a desire to pos-
ss a figure of Miss Nightingale—and
ly one nurse who already owned one
ho could be persuaded to part with it.

In the collection of Miss Elizabeth Johnson

Plate 45 'John Brown' (raised capitals). Unknown potter. c. 1859. Height 11½
'Uncle Tom & Eva'. Unknown potter. c. 1852. Height 11½"

John Brown (1800–1859), ardent abolitionist of slavery, was born in Connect
cut. In 1859, two years before the American Civil War, he led an abortive attack c
the Federal Arsenal at Harper's Ferry. He was captured and hanged.

Uncle Tom's Cabin by Harriet Beecher Stowe, published nine years before th
war, aroused intense sympathy amongst Abolitionists. Episodes from the boc
were the subject of many music-fronts. One by Louisa Corbaux is certainly th
source of a group titled 'Topsy & Eva'.

Other Staffordshire figures which are popular because of their American associ
tions include Captain Cook, Benjamin Franklin, Thomas Jefferson, Abraha
Lincoln and George Washington.

62

Plate 46 'S. O'Brien' (indented capitals). 'Alpha' Factory. c. 1848. Height 7″
  William Smith O'Brien (1803–1864) M.P. for County Limerick, was condemned
o death for high treason in 1848 but eventually transported to Tasmania, where
ne was pardoned in 1854. (See page 60.)

Plate 47 'Sheepshearer' (raised capitals). Unknown potter. c. 1852. Height $13\frac{3}{4}$
Another subject, like O'Brien and Captain Cook, much sought after by Austra
lians. It derives from a print by George Baxter, who patented a method of printing
in oil colours in 1836, titled 'News From Home', its companion print is 'New
From Australia'. The texture of the sheep's wool is obtained by painting the smooth
surfaces with slip and sprinkling it with granulated clay.

ate 48 'Grapplers' (raised capitals). Unknown potter. c. 1862. Height 11½″;
'thello & Iago' (raised capitals). Unknown potter. c. 1858. Height 12″

The Grapplers are based on a group in bronzed-zinc modelled by J. P. Molin
hich was lent by Sweden to the London International Exhibition of 1862. It
ow stands in front of the National Museum in Stockholm. The source of Othello
Iago is a water colour by S. A. Hart, R.A., exhibited at the Royal Academy in
58 and now in the Victoria and Albert Museum.

Fine portrait figures always command high prices but these groups, whilst
ither represents real people, have both brought record prices in auction. The
st time we bought an example of the Grapplers was in Bermondsey Market. It
st £7 and sold for treble the value the same day. In 1962 it came up for sale
ain and again trebled its price, thus selling for an outrageous (at that time) sum.

1967 another copy fetched, in auction, more than double the 1962 figure, and
1969 the price had again doubled.

Similarly an Othello & Iago fetched 42 guineas in 1966—a record price for the
ne—even though it was badly damaged and had been filled with concrete, a
ethod of repair which prevents any further effort to improve it. In 1969 a fine
rsion of the same group brought four times that price and later in the year an
ferior example sold for more again.

Plate 49 Horse. Unknown potter. c. 1760. Height 5″

Many collections of Staffordshire figures are composed entirely of anima
Whilst some collectors specialize in the type of dog they own, or breed—dalm
tions, greyhounds, spaniels, poodles, pugs or whippets—cat-lovers acquire ca
and hunters accumulate gun-dogs, deer or foxes.

Other collectors widen the scope by including all animals, domestic or wild; ar
the resultant menageries are both decorative and delightful. It would be almc
impossible to mention any animal which has not been captured in pottery at or
time or another. Birds, fish, reptiles, rodents and those groups representing circ
artists performing with, or other people being killed by, animals of various kin
are not excluded from this category.

Plate 50 Flatback Lion. Unknown potter. c. 1830. Height 13″

The immediate reaction of most people upon seeing a piece like this is that it is made of metal which has been painted. So many items of this type were made as door-stoppers that the supposition is not surprising. Ceramic items in this form are extremely rare. I know of a Mr. Punch (but no Judy) and only seven other smaller items in the same form. They are sometimes referred to as 'slice-groups'. The lion may have a unicorn as its pair and was probably issued to commemorate the coronation of William IV.

Plate 51 'Wallace' & 'Nero' (impressed capitals). Obadiah Sherratt. c. 1830
Height 4½", Length 6½"

The lions illustrated above are included to show that it was not necessary to be
human to become a portrait figure! Some named animals are easily identified and
can be dated with confidence. These include Jumbo (c. 1882), an African elephant
which was a great favourite with visitors to the Zoo from 1865 to 1882 when, in
spite of public protests, he was sold to Barnum, the American *entrepreneur* who
also arranged the American tour of Jenny Lind (see Plate 43); and McGrath
and Pretender, two greyhounds, the first belonging to Lord Lurgan and the other
to Mr. Punchard, who were contenders for the Waterloo Cup (for coursing) in
1871. Master McGrath was the victor and his deeds were celebrated in song and
ballad throughout the country.

Both in the collection of Miss Jean Anderson

I am indebted to Miss Hannah Winter, a notable researcher into the history of the circus, for the following information, loosely quoted from a letter:

'Henri Martin, who played Paris in 1831 and then went to London, had two lions named Néron and Cobourg. There are many penny-plains and two-pence-coloureds of him. Almost all lion trainers have a Nero—and usually a Sultan and Rajah. But my bet is on James Carter, who had belonged to Wombwell's Menagerie and was hired by William Batty for Astley's. It is the lion named Wallace which makes me think of Carter because he was a Scot.'

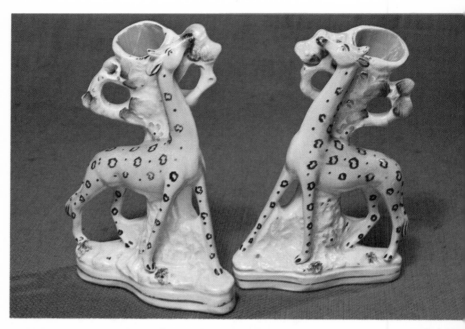

Plate 52 Giraffes. Unknown potter. c. 1840. Height 5½"
The first giraffe arrived in England in 1827, too early to be the inspiration of the figures illustrated here. But, in 1836, four others arrived at the Zoological Gardens and the first foal was born in 1840—a date which is both probable and acceptable ceramically for these figures.

Plate 53 Horses. Unknown potter. c. 1840. Height 5½"
The horses, sleek and superb in their coats of underglaze black, have passed through our hands in decorations which proclaim them to be cinnamon, dappled, piebald, skewbald, pure white and even striped to represent zebras.

All in the collection of Mr. & Mrs. Brian Rix

Plate 54 Two pairs of birds. Unknown potters. c. 1840. Heights 5"
Birds, represented singularly, even when the many representations of eagles made for the American market are included, are much rarer than any other forms of fauna made by the Staffordshire potters.

The smaller pair in the collection of Mrs. S. H. Proudford

Busts

A superb and interesting collection can be formed from busts alone. I have already mentioned some issued by Ralph Wood Junior and remarked upon Enoch Wood's sculptural ability which was used to great advantage on many busts he modelled. Obadiah Sherratt and William Chambers Junior of the South Wales Pottery, are also known to have produced busts but the majority, like all items of the period, are unmarked and may be the work of any number of potters.

The same caution must be exercised when purchasing busts as in the case of figures. William Kent's 1901 catalogue lists busts of The Madonna, Homer, Plato, Wesley, Alexander, Locke, Washington, Shakespeare and Britannia and the same list is in the last catalogue issued by William Kent (Porcelains) Ltd., in 1955. All these busts were originally modelled by Enoch Wood—Britannia is, in reality, his Minerva. The reproductions are notorious for badly defined features and the details, such as medals, orders and epaulettes, are more often painted on than present in the mould. They are thickly and garishly enamelled, the bases are often crudely painted to represent marble and they sometimes have passages of 'Bright Gold', a liquid preparation introduced in the early 1880s by Messrs. Johnson, Matthey & Co. This has a harsh brilliance quite unlike 'Best (or mercuric) Gold' always used before this date.

Busts, too, offer many topics in which to specialize. Literature, for example, represented by playwrights, poets, philosophers and scientists, includes busts of Lord Byron, John Milton, Alexander Pope, Matthew Prior, Shakespeare, Socrates and Voltaire. Military subjects include General Sir Ralph Abercromby, Lord Clive of India, Florence Nightingale and the Duke of Wellington; whilst amongst naval ones are Admirals Lords Duncan, Hood, Nelson and Rodney. Mythology is represented by Apollo, Hercules, Minerva, Neptune and Venus.

Political busts include George Canning, Richard Cobden, Charlotte Corday (the murderess of Marat), Earl Grey, Henry Hunt, Daniel O'Connell, Sir Robert Peel, Wellington (as a statesman) and George Washington. Religion, apart from over a hundred different busts of the Reverend John Wesley which alone would provide a lifetime's collecting, offers Jesus Christ, The Virgin Mary (Madonna in the Kent lists), the Reverends William Clowes, William Thorn and George Whitfield.

There are many busts of royal personages including King George III, Queen Caroline, Princess Charlotte and Prince Leopold; King William IV and his Queen Adelaide; Alexander, Tsar of Russia and Napoleon I, the Empress Josephine, the son, who was briefly King of Rome and Napoleon's brother, Joseph Buonaparte, whom he placed—for a short time—on the Spanish throne.

The stage and music offer fewer busts than one would expect and I can only record examples of Maria Foote (by Obadiah Sherratt), David Garrick, Edmund Kean, Jenny Lind and Sarah Siddons. I have, of course, confined this list to busts manufactured in earthenware and decorated in enamel glazes or coloured enamels. Many other examples are available in *bisque* or Parian, which are both types of unglazed porcelain.

Plate 55 *Right:* William IV. Obadiah
Sherratt. c. 1830. Height 8″

In the collection of Mr. Vern K. Miller

Plate 56 *Below left to right:* Minerva;
The Rev John Wesley; Alexander I,
Tsar of Russia. Wood & Caldwell.
c. 1812–1819. Heights 10½″ to 12″

Plaques

I have always had an intense dislike for domestic plates, no matter how rare or beautifully painted they are, which have been imprisoned in wire frames—with three or four ugly terminals overlapping the rims—and hung upon walls. Plates should be displayed on Welsh Dressers or in cabinets: they were, after all, manufactured for use and not for decoration. Plaques, which are always pierced for hanging, are pottery pictures intended to enrich the walls of houses where paintings could not be afforded. These days, of course, paintings are often less expensive than plaques!

Ranging in size from three to fourteen inches in width, height or diameter they are moulded in relief and the type of decoration—semi-translucent coloured glazes, underglaze or overglaze enamelling—is always an indication of their age. I have had examples of a plaque depicting a lady holding a bunch of grapes, from the same mould, in all three types of decoration mentioned. The fact that the design includes the Ralph Wood rebus mark of a group of trees might tempt the unwary to date it at the earliest period whereas the type of decoration used would indicate a later period.

Most plaques can be ascribed, again stylistically, to four schools—Whieldon, the Ralph Woods, Pratt and Enoch Wood. Signed pieces, the exception again proving the rule, are rare. When they are signed the proof of the potter is often worth a wager! I have had a plaque of two recumbent lions decorated in the superb semi-translucent coloured glazes of early Ralph Wood products and, except for the fact that it was impressed WEDGWOOD, I should have sold, and guaranteed it, as 'R. Wood c. 1760'. Another example, typical of those traditionally ascribed to William Pratt, was incised 'Thomas Kents, Burslem, Jan 24—1823'. This provides an earlier root to the Kent & Parr family tree than those recorded by either Balston or Godden!

The infinite variety of plaques is amazing. One may discover animals, battle scenes, biblical characters, birds, fish, flowers and fruit; lovers and scenes—both classical and rustic; portraits of actors, actresses, admirals, divines, explorers, generals, murderers, playwrights, philanthropists, philosophers, poets, politicians, royalty and saints as well as smokers, topers and traitors.

Lord Eccles writes in *On Collecting* that his plaques number almost two hundred and that he has only seen duplicates of about seventy of them even though he has searched the principal collections of Staffordshire pottery in museums as well as illustrations and references in books. He suggests, and is probably quite right, that most plaques were trial runs (or proof-pulls) for moulds which were intended to be used on domestic wares. I must admit that I have seen very few duplicates of the many plaques which have passed through my hands but I have often had examples from the same moulds on jugs, mugs and tea-caddies.

Plate 57 Charles I and Oliver Cromwell. Pratt Ware. ?c. 1800. Heights 7¼″
The engraving '(Wale delin. Roberts sculp.)' on nineteenth-century paper from a
book with a title I have failed to discover.

This pair of plaques provides more confirmation of the fact that every piece of
pottery has, somewhere, its source expressed in a print which was easily available
to the potter. Confined, as he was, in the provinces, he was obliged to rely upon
current publications to provide him with inspiration to tempt the public.

It is only possible to presume a date from these items and this is based upon the
fact that Charles was born in 1600 and died in 1649. His murderer, in truth if not
in execution of the deed, Oliver Cromwell, was one year younger and lived nine
years longer than the martyred King.

Whilst one can imagine a patriotic potter wishing to commemorate the bi-
centenary of Charles's birth it seems likely that one who was celebrating that of the
regicide would have shown the King less regal and Cromwell less apologetic.
Cromwell's glum face, and the remorse expressed in the gesture of his right hand
is a theatrical convention which equally expresses the phrases, 'I couldn't help it',
'It wasn't my fault' or 'I didn't know what I was doing'.

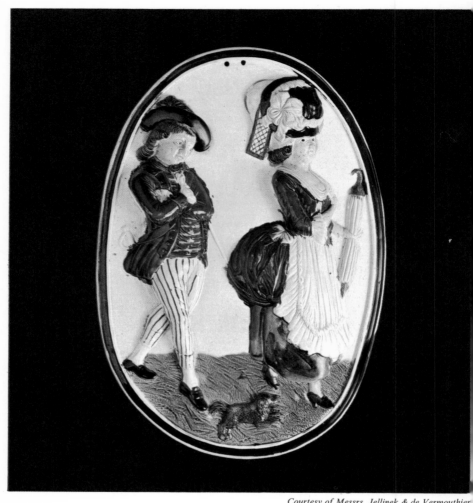

Plate 58 Plaque. Variously known as 'Patricia and her Lover' or 'Jack on a Cruise'. Ralph Wood Junior. c. 1770. Height 13¾"

late 59 Pair of plaques. Patricia's
over, or Jack; and Patricia, or a lady
f easy virtue. Ralph Wood Junior.
1700. Heights $8\frac{1}{8}''$ and $9\frac{5}{8}''$

The choice of these three items, a
uplication of subject, is to point the
act that the pairing of two plaques can
e justified even though they differ in
ize. In this case the difference is caused
y perspective. The sailor is in the back-
round of the plaque where they appear
ogether so he is smaller than the lovely
ady luring him to indescribable temp-
ations. Staffordshire potters were no-
oriously frugal, using only as much of
heir basic commodity, clay, as was
bsolutely necessary. So the fact that
he lover, on his own, is on a much
maller plaque than the one enclosing
atricia, is not a matter of great
mportance.

In the collection of Mr. Charles Smart

77

Plate 60 David Garrick. ?Ralp Wood Junior. c. 1780. Height 7¾″

Unsurpassed in both tragic and com rôles, David Garrick (1717–1779), wa certainly the most versatile actor in th history of the British stage. He made h début at Ipswich in 1741 and his fir London appearance, at Goodman Fields on October 9th of the same yea was sensational. His portrayal Richard III drew so many people tha the owners of the Patent Theatre alarmed by the loss of their audience invoked the Licensing Act of 1837 an had the theatre in Goodmans Field closed. Garrick was secured by th management of Drury Lane where except for one season at Covent Gai den, he remained until his retiremer in 1776. He instituted many reform one of the most important being th introduction of historical costume, sui able to the period of the play, instead the contemporary clothes then nor mally worn.

Plate 61 Sarah Siddons. Pratt Ware c. 1790. Height 8¾″

Sarah Siddons (1755–1831) was en gaged by Garrick for the Drury Lan season of 1775–1776. She was a failur and retired back to the provinces. I October 1782, she returned to Drur Lane in triumph and from then, unt she retired from the stage in 1812, he name dominated the British theatrica world.

SELECT BIBLIOGRAPHY

BALSTON, Thomas, O.B.E., M.C., *Victorian Staffordshire Portraits* in *Country Life Annual*, London 1951

—— *Staffordshire Portrait Figures of the Victorian Age*, Faber, London, 1958

—— *Supplement to Staffordshire Portrait Figures of the Victorian Age*, John Hall, Faber, London, 1963

EARLE, Cyril, *The Earle Collection of Early Staffordshire Pottery*, 1915

ECCLES, The Rt. Hon. Viscount, K.C.V.O., *On Collecting*, Longmans, Green, London, 1968
Lord Eccles writes here, and so happily, about motives for collecting, how to collect and how much pleasure he has gained by being a collector that one cannot imagine any reader of it not immediately looking round for something to collect.

GODDEN, Geoffrey A., F.R.S.A., *Victorian Portrait Figures* in *The Pottery Gazette and Glass Trade Review*, London, May 1963

—— *Encyclopaedia of British Pottery and Porcelain Marks*, Herbert Jenkins, London 1968; Crown, New York, 1968

—— *The Illustrated Encyclopaedia of British Pottery and Porcelain*, Herbert Jenkins, London, 1966, Crown, New York, 1969

HAGGAR, R. G., *Staffordshire Chimney Ornaments*, Phoenix House, London, 1955

LATHAM Bryan, C.B.E., *Victorian Staffordshire Portrait Figures for the Small Collector*, Tiranti, London, 1953; Transatlantic, U.S.A.

LEWIS, Griselda, *A Picture History of English Pottery*, Hulton Press, London, 1956
This, the classic example of a well-illustrated book, covers the development of English pottery from the Stone Age to the present day.

—— *A Collector's History of English Pottery*, Studio Vista, London, 1969

MANDER, Raymond, MITCHENSON, Joe, *A Picture History of The British Theatre*, Hulton Press, London, 1957

PUGH, P.D., O.B.E., F.R.S.A., *Staffordshire Portrait Figures and Allied Subjects of the Victorian Era*, Barrie & Jenkins, London, 1971; Praeger, New York, 1971

STANLEY, Louis T. *Collecting Staffordshire Pottery*, W. H. Allen, London, 1963